College Success:
A Focus on the First Year

Sally Lipsky & Stacey Winstead

Indiana University of Pennsylvania

D1525754

KENDALL/HUNT PUBLISHING COMPANY
4050 Westmark Drive   Dubuque, Iowa 52002

Dedication

*To my parents, Merle & Irene, who lovingly instilled in me
the importance of a college education.   ~S.A.L.*

*For my girls—Aja, Maya, and Olivia.
~S.C.W.*

College Success: A Focus on the First Year

Table of Contents

CHAPTER 1: Getting Acquainted   **page**

A Profile of You & Other Freshmen _____ *1*

Challenges for Your First Year _____ *3*

High School versus College _____ *5*

Application Assignment – Chapter 1 _____ *7*

CHAPTER 2: Making the 'Right' Decisions

College Success – Making the 'Right' Decisions _____ *9*

Becoming an Active Student _____ *10*

Characteristics of Active Decision-Making _____ *12*

Four Key Decisions _____ *13*

    Time to STOP and Reflect _____ *15*

Observing Active versus Passive Behaviors & Attitudes _____ *16*

Checklist for Active Decision-Making _____ *18*

Application Assignment – Chapter 2 _____ *19*

CHAPTER 3: Managing Your Time

Managing Your Time _____ *21*

Time Management – A Three-Step Process _____ *22*

Application Assignment – Chapter 3 _____ *25*

Common Time Management Objections & Myths _____ *27*

A Model Study Desk: Organization & Contents _____ *28*

CHAPTER 4: Planning Your Course of Studies

Becoming Familiar with Terminology _____ *29*

List of Institutional Contacts _____ *31*

Organization of a University _____ *32*

Academic Requirements: An Open Book Quiz _____ *33*

Beginning Your Curriculum Plan _____ *34*

    Time to STOP and Reflect _____ *36*

CHAPTER 5: Developing Study Strategies

Study Reading _____ 37

Application Assignment – Study Reading _____ 41

Lecture Note Taking _____ 46

Application Assignment – Lecture Note Taking _____ 47

CHAPTER 6: Connecting with the Campus Community

The Importance of 'Connecting' _____ 49

Types of Connections _____ 50

Exploring Campus Organizations _____ 52

Professors as Resources _____ 54

CHAPTER 7: Examining Policies & Procedures

Focus Questions: Student Policies _____ 57

    Academic Good Standing _____ 58

    Grading & Attendance Policies _____ 59

    Withdrawal Policy _____ 60

    Academic Integrity Policy _____ 61

    Student Behavior Standards _____ 62

    Alcohol Policy _____ 63

    Hazing Policy _____ 64

    Judicial Systems _____ 65

      Time to STOP and Reflect _____ 67

CHAPTER 8: Solving Problems & Setting Goals

Steps for Solving Problems: Case Studies _____ 69

Developing Personal Goals _____ 71

Evaluating Your Goals _____ 72

Goal Statements – 6 Steps _____ 73

Goal Statements – 4 Steps _____ 75

Application Assignment – Chapter 8 _____ 77

CHAPTER 9: A Focus on the Future _____ 79

Principles for College Success _____ 80

Preface

This text orients entering college students to the system of higher education and to the skills that promote effective educational planning.

Topics covered are:

⇨ The transition into higher education, including an overview of the organization of institutions and the academic and personal expectations placed on college students.

⇨ Decision-making issues, including a model of active involvement, time management techniques, reading and note taking strategies, and goal setting.

⇨ Selected issues in college student adjustment, including problem solving strategies, academic policies and procedures, and students' responsibilities.

⇨ Curriculum overview, including useful terminology, liberal studies or core curriculum requirements, and major/minor requirements.

⇨ Academic and personal assessment and planning.

⌔ **The text is intended to be used as an active learning _workbook_. By completing a series of structured, detailed activities and assignments, readers will demonstrate both an _understanding_ and _application_ of the concepts covered.**

The workbook has these distinct advantages:

⇨ **Core topics that are immediately relevant to first-year college students.**

⇨ **A student-centered focus with practical, hands-on activities.**

⇨ **A variety of collaborative, problem-solving activities.**

⇨ **Assignments using campus resources that introduce students to:**

  • Writing center and tutorial services.

  • Computer labs, e-mail procedures, and student technology services.

  • Major/minor departments, academic advisors, and professors.

  • Student organizations.

  • Individual and group study locations.

⇨ **An accompanying _First-Year Planner_ that includes**:

- Calendars, schedules, and to-do lists for the academic year, July→June.

- Checklist to assess active decision-making throughout the year.

⇨ **A great deal of flexibility for use within freshman-year programming**, including:

- Pre-college experiences of short duration (a week or less).

- Multi-week summer bridge programs.

- Semester-long freshman module courses.

- Non-credit workshops.

⇨ **An accompanying _Instructor's Guide_ providing**:

- Detailed teaching directions and recommendations for each activity.

- Suggestions for enhancing content.

- Sample course syllabus or outline.

- Sample course or program evaluation instrument.

⇨ **A very _moderate price._**

The authors gratefully acknowledge the work of the following professional colleagues and office staff who assisted with this text in a variety of ways:
Susan Allshouse, Carmy Carranza, Beverly Johnson, Jessica Mayhugh, and Rosemarie Rearick.

CHAPTER 1: Getting Acquainted

A Profile of You and Other Freshmen

Welcome to the beginning of your college career. The activities in this workbook are designed to better prepare you for the many and varied personal, social, and intellectual changes – and challenges – you likely will be experiencing during your first year of college.

Your answers to the following questions will provide a means by which your instructor and your classmates can begin to know you. Be <u>honest</u> and <u>precise</u> with your responses, keeping in mind that your answers will be shared with others in the class.

1. **Why did you choose this college? Was this institution your first choice? If not, where did you prefer to go to college?**

2. **What is your academic major? Why did you choose this major? What do you hope to do with a degree in this major?**

3. **Where are you from – what community and state?**

4. **List three words or phrases that accurately describe you *or* identify something about yourself that others would not know just by looking at you.**

5. **What do you expect that you will be doing ten years from now?**

A Profile of You and Other Freshmen
— Side Two —

✔ Check with your instructor – this might be a group assignment.

After completing your answers to the questions on the front side of the page...

1) **Turn to a classmate – explain your answers to your classmate, and vice versa.**

2) **You and your partner combine with other students to form a larger group. Each person introduces his/her partner, using information just learned about that classmate.**

3) **Summarize what you found out about others in your group – do any patterns emerge?**

4) **Each group reports their summaries to the entire class.**

[Use this page for notes.]

Challenges for Your First Year

	As you begin your first year of college, indicate your biggest concern, or challenge, about...	Examine your Syllabus or Outline & the Table of Contents for this text→ Will your concern be covered in this course or program? Where?
College Academic Life:		
College Social Life:		
Your Personal Life:		

At the END of the course or program indicate...

	What you have learned about your initial concern or challenge.	*What **burning question** you still have.*
College Academic Life:		
College Social Life:		
Your Personal Life:		

High School versus College

For each item, write what you experienced in high school and what you *expect* in college.

	High School	College
Class Schedule:		
In-Class Work: **- Lectures & Notes** **- Group Work**		
Attendance:		
Out-of-Class Work: **- Reading** **- Papers/Projects**		
Tests:		

Studying:
  When –
  Where –
  How Much –		

Amount of Effort:		
Texts & Supplies:		
Grades/Standards:		
Continued….		

	High School	College
Instructors:		
Parents' Involvement:		
Meals:		
Social Life:		
Sleep:		
Financial Obligations:		
Responsibilities:		
Independence:		

In 2-4 sentences, <u>summarize</u> the major differences between high school & college:

Application Assignment – Chapter 1

✓ Check with your instructor – this might be a Writing Center assignment.

The Discovery Paper

Concept: *An Examination of Your Decision to Attend College*
[Hopefully, this examination will encourage you to examine *all* significant decisions you make about your future].

Purpose:
- First, to provide an exploration of *why* you are attending college. The assignment guides you in determining how your decision to attend college will shape your future endeavors.
- Second, to provide a meaningful writing experience through a personalized essay style. This is an opportunity for you to use the campus Writing Center or word processing labs.

Instructions:
1. Type your answers to the three questions listed below. (At least two paragraphs for each question, or 1 ½ - 2 pages, double-spaced.)

2. Write in complete sentences and paragraphs. Organize your thoughts, ideas, and sentences in a coherent manner.

3. After completing the assignment, identify briefly (in 1-3 sentences) why this assignment was worthwhile for you.

4. Optional: Discuss briefly any problems or difficulties you had while completing this assignment.

Questions:

➢ **What key factors were involved in your decision to attend college?**

➢ **What advantages in life do you believe exist for someone who chooses to attend college contrasted to someone who chooses <u>not</u> to attend college? Are there any advantages for someone who chooses not to attend college?**

➢ **How will college impact your future (short-term or long-term) goals and plans?**

Evaluating Your Discovery Paper

The following criteria will be used in evaluating your final paper. Use this information when writing and revising your work.

Content: Provide information that is clear, specific, and represents a full understanding of the assignment. Avoid vague answers and one-sentence paragraphs.

Organization: Organize the assignment in a cohesive and orderly fashion with paragraphs connecting to produce a well-developed essay. Avoid sentences that are not specific or move from one point to another with little clarification.

Grammar/Style/Mechanics: Make sure you spell words correctly, have no run-on sentences, have no sentence fragments, and use correct subject and verb agreement.

Instructions: Follow all instructions indicated on the assignment sheet for maximum points in this section.

✔ Check with your instructor regarding specific point values for this assignment.

Point value for each section = _____.   Total maximum points = _____.

1. **Give your paper to a classmate to read and evaluate, or reread it yourself. In the chart below record your rating or point value for each of the areas.**
   - ❑ Do you want to make changes before turning in this assignment?

2. **After receiving your instructor's evaluation of your paper, record the point values.**
   - ❑ What are the differences between the two ratings?
   - ❑ What did you discover about how you approach writing assignments?
   - ❑ What did you discover about your writing skills – your strengths & weaknesses?
   - ❑ What do you intend to do differently for your next writing assignment?

Evaluation Criteria	Rating by Self _or_ Peer	Rating by Instructor
Content:		
Organization:		
Grammar/Style/Mechanics:		
Instructions:		
Total Score:		

CHAPTER 2: Making the 'Right' Decisions

College Success – Making the 'Right' Decisions

hat activity are you successful at doing? Write this activity below. Then consider *why* you are successful at this activity. List two or three key personal *actions* or *attitudes* that explain why you are successful with this activity. Examples from other college students are included.

I am successful at:

WHY?

Examples:

I.   I am successful at tennis because I've spent many, many hours practicing the sport. Also, I had a good coach (my father) to help me with the techniques of the sport. Also, I enjoy playing tennis—especially when I win!!

II.   I am successful at crossword puzzles for several reasons. First, I am good with words and different meanings. Second, I have much experience since I do a puzzle everyday in the newspaper. Third, since I only feel satisfied if I complete the entire puzzle, my goal is to finish the entire puzzle.

III.   I am successful at helping other people. One reason is because I am a good listener. Also, I am an optimist and people tell me that I convey that spirit to others. I'm motivated to help others because it makes me feel good to see other people benefit from my advice.

1)   **In the examples, what common characteristics do you notice among the students?**

2)   **What elements have led to their successes for their varied activities?**

3)   **Can you draw parallels to those factors that led to your success with an activity?**

Your successes, as well as those of the college students mentioned above, can be applied to the academic demands of college. Most students feel a sense of satisfaction, accomplishment, and even enjoyment when they perform well in a course. You will want to perform well your first year of college by transferring the behaviors and attitudes used for other successful activities into your daily academic life. You are beginning your college career – from this point on you will be making daily decisions about what you do in <u>and</u> out of the classroom. These decisions will directly and immediately affect how successful and satisfied you are with college life.

🔑   **Your attitudes and actions will affect your level of success in <u>each</u> course that you will be enrolled in this year.**

Becoming an Active Student

✓ Check with your instructor – this might be a group assignment.

<u>**Read about the two students, noting differences in decisions – and consequences – for each:**</u>

I.   Tim enters his room in the residence hall. It is 9:00 p.m. on Thursday. Tim flops on his bed and opens his biology notebook to begin studying for the Friday morning quiz. The phone rings; Tim answers it and talks to his friend Andy about meeting at the fraternity mixer Friday night. No sooner does Tim put the receiver down, than his neighbor Shawn comes to Tim's open door to chat about Saturday's softball tournament. After Shawn leaves, Tim tries to concentrate but is distracted by the loud music being played in the hallway. A few minutes later Tim's roommate comes into the room and turns on the TV to watch <u>E.R.</u> Closing his biology notebook, Tim watches the show with his roommate.

II.   Mara enters the large psychology classroom, walking towards her customary seat in the front. She passes several acquaintances from her residence hall, who ask Mara to sit with them in the back of the room. Mara declines, saying that she will see them after class. After quickly taking her seat, Mara opens her notebook and reviews what had been covered during the last class session. The lecture begins. Mara selects important ideas the professor emphasizes to write in her notebook, leaving generous spaces in case she needs to fill in missing points or clarifying examples when she reviews her notes that evening. She answered a question the professor asked the class. Once, when she was unclear about a point the professor was making, Mara raised her hand and asked him to for an example. Throughout the lecture, Mara kept her psychology textbook open so that she could highlight parts of the chapter that the professor was talking about. At the end of the class, Mara approached her professor to tell him that she was still uncertain about a concept – she asked to meet with him. The professor made an appointment to see Mara for the next day. After jotting the time in her weekly planner, Mara ran to catch up with her friends.

| | TIM: | | MARA: |
Decision	Consequence	Decision	Consequence

Who is the more "active" student?   **Why?**

Who is the more "passive" student?   **Why?**

Making the "right" decisions for yourself requires an "active" approach to your college education. Being conscientious, responsible, self-directed, and persistent when dealing with academic, social, and personal issues will result in more positive and rewarding consequences for yourself.

Characteristics of Active Decision-Making

✔ Check with your instructor – this might be a group assignment.

How would you describe 'active decision-making'?
In the space below, list 4-5 components of active decision-making in the context of college life.

Examples: "Students make deliberate choices about when to study."
"Students carefully decide about the importance of social events."

Now, *revise* Tim's scenario to reflect a model of "Active Decision-Making."

TIM:

Revised Decision _____ *New* Consequence

Four Key Decisions

✔ Check with your instructor – this might be an e-mail assignment.

Refer to the chart, *High School vs. College* (pages 5-6). Given the characteristics of your upcoming freshman year, what key decisions do you anticipate making if you are to excel academically? List four decisions that will be important for you this upcoming year.

1.

2.

3.

4.

Making the "right" decisions will involve much commitment, hard work, and trial-and-error on your part. As you accumulate personal successes in your college-level coursework, notice the sense of confidence and well being that builds within you.

Put Yourself in the Cycle of Academic Success:

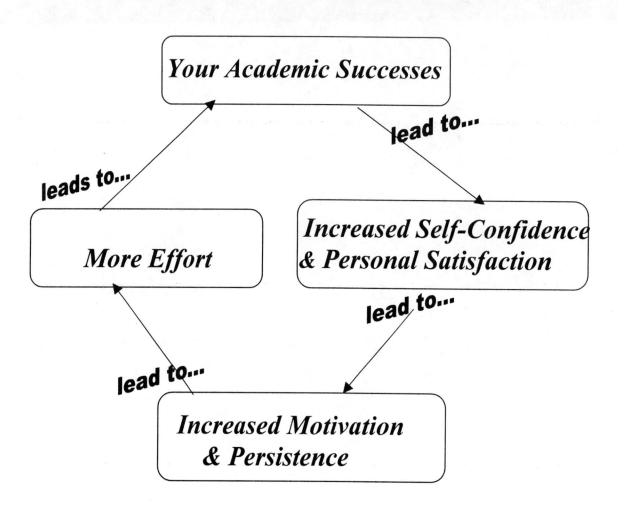

Your Academic Successes

lead to...

Increased Self-Confidence & Personal Satisfaction

lead to...

Increased Motivation & Persistence

lead to...

More Effort

leads to...

Time to ...

...and reflect.

Complete the following items:

A. Write a *burning question* that you have at this point.

B. In 2-3 sentences summarize the *most useful information* you have learned up to this point.

Observing Active versus Passive Behaviors & Attitudes

✓ Check with your instructor – this likely is a homework assignment.

Jot down **active** and **passive** *behaviors* and *attitudes* of your peers. That is, what do you see your peers *doing* or *saying* that reflects either an **active** or **passive** orientation towards personal, social, and/or academic life. Examples are:

Active: 1) Asks for directions to an unknown building, **2)** Decides to study early in the evening when he/she is freshest, **3)** Participates in class or talks to the professor in an effort to make the subject interesting.

Passive: 1) Follows other students to an unknown building, **2)** Waits to study when roommate studies, **3)** Complains that the professor or class was boring.

Assignment #1

ACTIVE	versus	PASSIVE

✓ Check to see if behaviors you observed your peers doing are on the
Checklist for Active Decision-Making (page 18).

Assignment #2:

ACTIVE	versus	PASSIVE

Assignment #3:

ACTIVE	versus	PASSIVE

Checklist for Active Decision-Making

#1) Which items have you done since entering college? Check those items in Column # 1.
#2) Which items are new to you? Check those items in Column #2.
#3) Which items do you need more information about? Check those items in Column #3.

	#1 I've done this.	#2 This is new to me.	#3 Need more info.
1. Am I studying *regularly* throughout the week?			
2. Am I studying in a location free of distractions?			
3. Am I using a planner or calendar to write down class assignments, due dates, appointments, meetings, etc.			
4. Am I making priority lists of what I have to do each day?			
5. Am I doing some type of preparation *before* each class, such as reading text material and/or reviewing notes?			
6. Am I asking questions when I don't understand or when I'm not sure?			
7. Am I *thinking* as I take notes in class?			
8. Am I reviewing and organizing my lecture notes *after* each class, while the information is still fresh in my mind?			
9. Am I pacing my reading for each course, reading in chunks of time when I am freshest?			
10. Am I making some type of study guide for my reading, such as highlighting and marking the text, summary notes, study cards, or developing practice test questions?			
11. Am I utilizing academic support services such as Tutoring, Writing Center, Supplemental Instruction, & workshops?			
12. Am I meeting with my professor for *each subject* to discuss my performance?			
13. Am I allowing extra time the week before a test in order to prepare adequately?			
14. Am I utilizing campus support services such as the Counseling Center, Career Services, Financial Aid, and the Health Center?			
15. Am I involved in extracurricular activities, including student organizations & clubs, volunteer campus & community services, sports, and campus work study?			
16. Am I associating with other students who are responsible, supportive, and doing well academically?			

This Checklist is reproduced in the accompanying Planner in order for you to review your progress.

Application Assignment – Chapter 2

You – as a Learner!

Write an in-depth description of yourself as a learner. Complete all three of the following essay questions.

1. **Are you a *passive* learner or an *active* learner?**

2. **Describe your learning behaviors using concrete details and examples that explain *how you approach a learning task* and *how much time you spend on task*.**

3. **Choose one statement to complete:**
    "I will incorporate active learning behaviors by...."
            OR
    "I will further enhance the use of active learning strategies by...."

CHAPTER 3: Managing Your Time

A major difference between high school and college is the amount of *freedom* that students experience daily in college. In college, administrators will not schedule back-to-back classes for you, instructors will not check your class attendance, and parents will not monitor your daily homework assignments. Instead, you will be able to choose not only which subjects to take, but also whether to go to class at all! You will decide whether to study or to watch a favorite TV program, whether to review for a test or to socialize with friends. Of course, the result of your daily decisions will be revealed at semester's end when final grades arrive in the mail!

This newfound freedom occurs within the context of increasing personal *and* academic responsibilities. As a college student, you likely are – or soon will be – juggling a variety of academic tasks, personal chores, and social changes, and financial commitments. As a result, **managing your time <u>effectively</u> is probably the greatest challenge you will face as a first-year college student!**

The following supplies are essential tools for organizing your days and ensuring productive use of both your academic and social time:

   🔑 The First-Year Planner that accompanies this text contains all *three* of the following supplies.

♦ **Calendar:** A calendar for the semester will provide you with an overview of the upcoming months. You will be able to plan ahead and pace yourself for the upcoming term when you jot down these key dates on your calendar:
1. *Organization of each term or semester* – starting and ending dates, mid-term dates, college breaks, reading day and final exams period, etc.
2. *Other academic dates and deadlines* – drop/add period, withdrawal, scheduling, payments, financial applications, etc.
3. *Important class dates* – quizzes, exams, papers, & projects as outlined in the syllabus.

♦ **Weekly Planner:** A planner will provide you with an overview of a week's assignments, activities, and other obligations. Get a planner that is compact and convenient enough to carry with you throughout the day for ready reference. Consider a weekly planner as an *essential* item – it provides the backbone for how you structure your time, pace yourself, and complete your tasks. As a college student, it is up to *you* to remember <u>where</u> you should be, at <u>what time</u> and <u>what place</u>, and with <u>what completed assignment</u>. A planner helps you to be aware of not only course assignments and tests, but also "special" commitments, such as a doctor's appointment, meeting with your advisor, or tutorial appointment. *Use of a planner will greatly reduce procrastination and stress in your day-to-day life at college.*

♦ **Daily Lists:** If you aren't yet a list-maker, become one! As you begin your freshman year, you will be inundated with a multitude of details throughout each day. Keep a small tablet of paper, note cards or sticky paper handy in which to *write down* these details as they arise. You are *much* less likely to forget, change, or put off tasks and obligations if you write them down. As the daily lists become longer, you can prioritize and order what you will accomplish, adding some tasks to your weekly planner or calendar. And you will enjoy crossing off each completed task on your list.

Time Management – A Three-Step Process

Step One – Creating Your Skeleton Schedule for the Semester

Begin by identifying all of your *set activities* for the semester. What *scheduled commitments* do you have that will not change from week to week? Examples include: classes, work, sport practice, club and affiliation meetings, and of course, sleeping and eating.

In the sample <u>Skeleton Schedule</u> below, note the open spaces of time available for other weekly activities. This especially is important if you assume that you will not have enough time in a day to accomplish all of your priorities. A <u>Skeleton Schedule</u> becomes a valuable visual aid.

Skeleton Schedule

Monday	Tuesday	Wednesday	Thursday	Friday	Saturday	Sunday
8:00-9:00 **History class**	8:00-9:00 **sleep**	8:00-9:00 **History class**	8:00-9:00 **sleep**	8:00-9:00 **History class**	8:00-9:00	8:00-9:00
9:00-10:00 **Biology class**	9:00-10:00 **get dressed/ breakfast**	9:00-10:00 **Biology class**	9:00-10:00 **dressed get/ breakfast**	9:00-10:00 **Biology class**	9:00-10:00	9:00-10:00
10:00-11:00	10:00-11:00	10:00-11:00	10:00-11:00 **Freshman Seminar class**	10:00-11:00	10:00-11:00	10:00-11:00
11:00-12:00	11:00-12:00	11:00-12:00	11:00-12:00	11:00-12:00	11:00-12:00 **weekly tennis lesson**	11:00-12:00 **attend church service**
12:00-1:00 **lunch**	12:00-1:00	12:00-1:00 **lunch**	12:00-1:00	12:00-1:00 **lunch**	12:00-1:00	12:00-1:00
1:00-2:00 **work**	1:00-2:00 **English class**	1:00-2:00 **work**	1:00-2:00 **English class**	1:00-2:00 **English class**	1:00-2:00 **weekly choir practice**	1:00-2:00
2:00-3:00 **work**	2:00-3:00 **lunch**	2:00-3:00 **work**	2:00-3:00 **lunch**	2:00-3:00	2:00-3:00	2:00-3:00
3:00-4:00 **work**	3:00-4:00 **Math class**	3:00-4:00 **work**	3:00-4:00 **Math class**	3:00-4:00	3:00-4:00	3:00-4:00
4:00-5:00	4:00-5:00	4:00-5:00	4:00-5:00 **Biology lab**	4:00-5:00	4:00-5:00	4:00-5:00
5:00-6:00	5:00-6:00	5:00-6:00	5:00-6:00 **Biology lab**	5:00-6:00	5:00-6:00	5:00-6:00
6:00-7:00	6:00-7:00	6:00-7:00	6:00-7:00 **dinner**	6:00-7:00	6:00-7:00	6:00-7:00
7:00-8:00	7:00-8:00	7:00-8:00	7:00-8:00	7:00-8:00	7:00-8:00	7:00-8:00
8:00-9:00	8:00-9:00	8:00-9:00	8:00-9:00	8:00-9:00	8:00-9:00	8:00-9:00
9:00-10:00	9:00-10:00	9:00-10:00	9:00-10:00	9:00-10:00	9:00-10:00	9:00-10:00
10:00-11:00	10:00-11:00	10:00-11:00	10:00-11:00	10:00-11:00	10:00-11:00	10:00-11:00
11:00-12:00 **get ready for bed**	11:00-12:00 **get ready for bed**	11:00-12:00 **get ready for bed**	11:00-12:00 **get ready for bed**	11:00-12:00	11:00-12:00	11:00-12:00

Step Two – Creating Your Weekly Schedule

A Weekly Schedule is your pre-determined plan for the semester. Identify tasks, commitments, and activities that you likely will have *every week*. In particular, consider *how much out-of-class study time* you will need *for each course*, and then reserve empty time slots for *when* you can best focus on that course. Be precise about what you plan to do; this will help you stay on task. For example, rather than write 'study' in an empty block, indicate *what subject* you plan on studying. An illustration of how a student's Skeleton Schedule is transformed into a Weekly Schedule follows. (*Italicized words* are the additions.) Your completed Weekly Schedule becomes your **guide** for the semester or term.

Weekly Schedule

Monday	Tuesday	Wednesday	Thursday	Friday	Saturday	Sunday
8:00-9:00 **History class**	8:00-9:00 sleep	8:00-9:00 **History class**	8:00-9:00 sleep	8:00-9:00 **History class**	8:00-9:00	8:00-9:00
9:00-10:00 **Biology class**	9:00-10:00 *get dressed/ breakfast*	9:00-10:00 **Biology class**	9:00-10:00 *get dressed/ breakfast*	9:00-10:00 **Biology class**	9:00-10:00	9:00-10:00
10:00-11:00 *review Biology notes*	10:00-11:00 *History – SI group tutorial*	10:00-11:00 *review Biology notes*	10:00-11:00 **Freshman Seminar class**	10:00-11:00 *review Biology notes*	10:00-11:00	10:00-11:00
11:00-12:00 *review History notes*	11:00-12:00	11:00-12:00 *review History notes*	11:00-12:00	11:00-12:00 *review History notes*	11:00-12:00 **weekly tennis lesson**	11:00-12:00 **attend church service**
12:00-1:00 lunch	12:00-1:00 *prepare for English*	12:00-1:00 lunch	12:00-1:00 *prepare for English*	12:00-1:00 lunch	12:00-1:00	12:00-1:00 *brunch w/ friends*
1:00-2:00 work	1:00-2:00 **English class**	1:00-2:00 work	1:00-2:00 **English class**	1:00-2:00 **English class**	1:00-2:00 **weekly choir practice**	1:00-2:00
2:00-3:00 work	2:00-3:00 lunch	2:00-3:00 work	2:00-3:00 lunch	2:00-3:00 *go to bank*	2:00-3:00	2:00-3:00
3:00-4:00 work	3:00-4:00 **Math class**	3:00-4:00 work	3:00-4:00 **Math class**	3:00-4:00 *do laundry*	3:00-4:00	3:00-4:00
4:00-5:00 *workout*	4:00-5:00 *do Math homework*	4:00-5:00 *workout*	4:00-5:00 **Biology lab**	4:00-5:00 *workout*	4:00-5:00	4:00-5:00
5:00-6:00 dinner	5:00-6:00 dinner	5:00-6:00 *Math Home-work Helper*	5:00-6:00 **Biology lab**	5:00-6:00 dinner	5:00-6:00	5:00-6:00
6:00-7:00	6:00-7:00	6:00-7:00 *dinner*	6:00-7:00 *dinner*	6:00-7:00	6:00-7:00 *club meeting*	6:00-7:00
7:00-8:00 *English homework*	7:00-8:00 *English homework*	7:00-8:00 *go to Writing Center*	7:00-8:00 *English homework*	7:00-8:00	7:00-8:00	7:00-8:00 *Prepare for upcoming*
8:00-9:00 *read History*	8:00-9:00 *read History*	8:00-9:00 *read History*	8:00-9:00 *History – SI group tutorial*	8:00-9:00	8:00-9:00	8:00-9:00 *week* ↓
9:00-10:00 *Biology homework*	9:00-10:00 *Biology homework*	9:00-10:00 *favorite TV show*	9:00-10:00 *Biology homework*	9:00-10:00 *go out with friends*	9:00-10:00 *go out with friends*	9:00-10:00
10:00-11:00 *Math homework*	10:00-11:00	10:00-11:00	10:00-11:00	10:00-11:00 ↓	10:00-11:00 ↓	10:00-11:00
11:00-12:00 *get ready for bed*	11:00-12:00 *get ready for bed*	11:00-12:00 *get ready for bed*	11:00-12:00 *get ready for bed*	11:00-12:00 ↓	11:00-12:00 ↓	11:00-12:00

Step Three – Creating Your Weekly/Daily 'Things-To-Do' List

Begin by determining your goals for the week. For academic goals, ask yourself the following question: "*What tasks should I complete in order to be adequately prepared for each class every day this week?*" You will find the answer to this question by regularly attending classes and following your course syllabi. This is a *weekly process* – refer to your Weekly Schedule for the days and times that you have available to complete these tasks. An example of a Weekly/Daily 'Things-To-Do' List follows:

Week 5 (of the semester)   Weekly/Daily Things-To-Do List

Monday	-read pages 46-60 of Biology text & take notes -brainstorm ideas for English paper -complete Math homework, pages 50-55
Tuesday	-write first draft of English paper -read pages 61-79 of Biology text & take notes -complete Math homework, pages 60-65
Wednesday	-schedule meeting with academic advisor -go to Writing Center for help with English paper -read chapter 4, Freshmen Seminar text
Thursday	-type up final draft of English paper -read pages 80-95 of Biology text & take notes
Friday	-turn in English paper -see academic advisor for pre-registration at 2pm -make flashcards for next week's History quiz
Saturday	-club meeting at 6pm
Sunday	-group study for History quiz -review Biology notes

Goals for Next Week:

1) Earn a 'B' or 'A' on History Quiz

2) Start reading next Biology chapter

3) Make an appointment with Math Professor & go to Homework Helper

✓ Check with your instructor – this might be a group assignment.

Answer the following questions:

1. **What should you *listen for & look for in class* to help you determine academic priorities for the week?**

2. **What should you *look for in each course syllabus* to help you determine academic priorities for the week?**

Application Assignment – Chapter 3

You will need your *First-Year Planner* for this assignment.

I. **Develop a <u>Skeleton Schedule</u> for yourself** (refer to page 22):

    1. On the first schedule labeled <u>Skeleton Schedule</u>, fill in your scheduled commitments for the semester. Again, these are your set activities for the term that will not change.

    2. There are two blank schedules labeled <u>Weekly Schedule</u> for each semester or term in the *First-Year Planner*. Use one of these schedules to change your personalized <u>Skeleton Schedule</u> into a standardized <u>Weekly Schedule</u>. The extra schedule is for any changes that might occur throughout the term.

II. **Develop a completed Weekly Schedule for yourself** (refer to p. 23) **for the term:** _____

III. **Develop a Weekly/Daily Things-To-Do List** (refer to page 24) **for the week of:** _____

    ❑ Keep all schedules handy for *ready referral*.

    ❑ Note any major changes that occur as you progress through the upcoming days, weeks, and semesters.

IV. **<u>Evaluate</u> how effective each schedule was for you by answering these questions:**

    1. **Was the (list, schedule) an appropriate tool for guiding how you used your time? Why or why not?**

    2. **What were the major changes that occurred? How did these changes affect you?**

    3. **Was the format appropriate?**

    4. **Will you use this type of schedule in the future? Why or why not?**

I made a weekly schedule to help me organize assignments & responsibilities that I had for the entire week. I found this a tremendous help because I was never caught off guard. It gave me the opportunity to work ahead of time. I kept my weekly schedule in my planner, next to my calendar. Using a weekly schedule is so helpful because I group all tasks and assignments together, as opposed to having them in separate folders. My daily schedule helps me organize my day and seize every minute of the day. Instead of waiting at the hairdresser for my appointment and reading a magazine, I took my reading assignment and finished almost the entire thing.

Before making these schedules I had much more wasted time. I will definitely use schedules for the rest of the semester. My stress level has dropped tremendously in just one week because I feel so much more organized. I feel on top of my assignments instead of overwhelmed. (Julie G.)

By making a schedule before my day starts, I get to see where I stand and what I need to accomplish. I depend on this schedule for structure. I usually find myself being distracted very easily. But, by creating a schedule and following it, I accomplished much more. (Kristen S.)

In the past, it was very easy for me to allow myself to be distracted and to take part in social activities. I would be studying, and then someone would come and ask me if I would like to play some hockey, or something similar to that scenario. Much more often that not, I would say, "Sure," without hesitating or even acknowledging that I have other responsibilities. Then, I tried a new technique. I started trying to manage my time better. I began to allot certain times for studying or doing homework, and sticking to them. Then if something better came up, it did not act as a distraction, but an incentive to finish my work. (Michael H.)

I posted the Skeleton Schedule beside my mirror, so that I could have easy access to it the entire week. Now I'm used to having it there, and it helps me to stay on track, so I'm going to leave it there for the entire semester. (Nicole B.)

Common Time Management Objections & Myths

 # 1: *"I do not need to write down what I have to do; I'll remember things in my head."*

If you write intentions down, you are <u>much more</u> likely to follow through with them. It is too easy to forget or distort intentions that are stored in the head, as opposed to those things written down for your constant review.

#2: *"It's impossible for me to use a schedule; I study when I'm in the mood."*

Like others, you no doubt have times when you feel like working and other times when you feel like playing. However, if you solely rely on your moods to dictate study time, often the "right" moods are few and far between, resulting in procrastination, little study time, and much stress. <u>You</u> are in control of your moods and feelings (and not vice versa!), and <u>you</u> are in control of when you want to direct yourself towards schoolwork. Think about those factors that make you in the mood to study and use these factors to your advantage – this will make you more in control of your college life. For example, if weather has a lot of influence on your studying, plan to study in the morning and evenings so that you have afternoons free to enjoy pleasant weather. Or, if the result of a daily phone conversation with your boyfriend or girlfriend determines your mood, study first and talk to him/her <u>after</u> your work is finished.

#3: *"A written schedule is too rigid for me."*

Schedules are <u>guidelines</u> for how you intend to spend your time. Allow for some flexibility within these guidelines. You can make your schedule – a calendar, weekly planner, and/or daily list—as specific or general as you please. ✐ **Experiment with how much structure you need in order to effectively manage your time, but <u>do</u> use some type of written schedule.**

#4: *"Developing a schedule takes too much time."*

If you have never developed any type of schedule for yourself, yes, you will have to devote time to organizing and writing down your intended activities. However, once you come up with a format that works for you, it takes little time to update or make changes to your schedule. Also, think of the payoff – organizing your day-to-day life can save much time in the long run.

#5: *"There is never enough time to accomplish all that is before me; I have too much to do!"*

Sometimes the demands of college seem overwhelming. Careful and deliberate daily attention to your time—via a calendar, weekly schedule/planner, and/or daily list – will help you overcome the frustrations of juggling multiple tasks.

If you are overwhelmed because you put things off until the last minute, regular use of schedules will help you triumph over *procrastination*. By identifying daily chunks of time to spend on a task, no matter how dreaded, you will be more likely to do it <u>now</u> instead of later. Daily work adds up to completion of tasks, both large and small. Over an extended period, the time you spend on multiple tasks will help you to turn <u>intentions</u> into <u>accomplished goals</u>.

Add any additional objections you may have.

A Model Study Desk:
Organization & Contents

Contributed by: Jessica Mayhugh

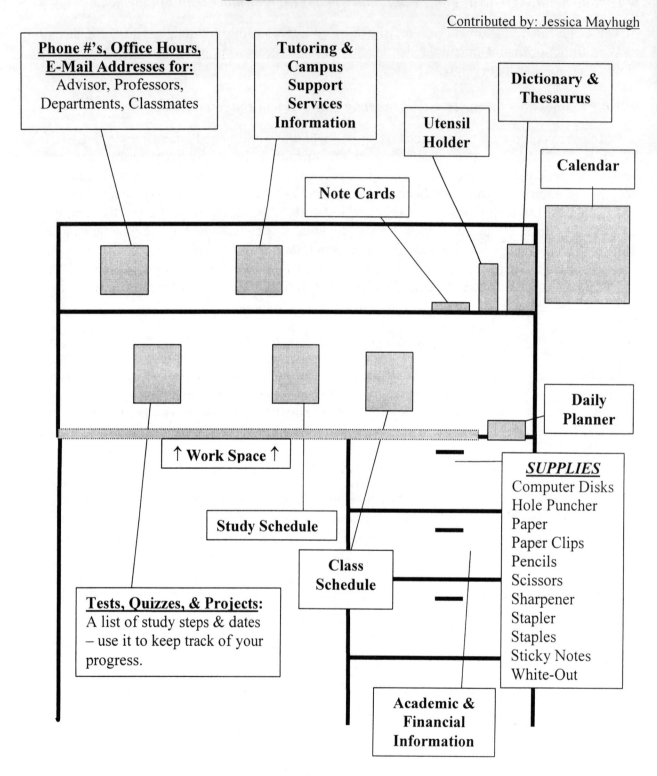

Phone #'s, Office Hours, E-Mail Addresses for: Advisor, Professors, Departments, Classmates

Tutoring & Campus Support Services Information

Dictionary & Thesaurus

Utensil Holder

Calendar

Note Cards

Daily Planner

↑ **Work Space** ↑

SUPPLIES
Computer Disks
Hole Puncher
Paper
Paper Clips
Pencils
Scissors
Sharpener
Stapler
Staples
Sticky Notes
White-Out

Study Schedule

Class Schedule

Tests, Quizzes, & Projects: A list of study steps & dates – use it to keep track of your progress.

Academic & Financial Information

CHAPTER 4: Planning Your Course of Studies

Becoming Familiar with Terminology

Explain what each term or abbreviation means. Use your undergraduate catalog, student handbook, and/or curriculum guide. *Why is each term important for you – when will you likely use the term?*

✔ Check with your instructor – this might be a group assignment.

1. Academic advisor

2. Academic good standing & Academic recovery

3. Academic probation

4. Block final exams & Cumulative final exams

5. Commuters

6. Course add/drop

7. Course repeat

8. Credit hours

9. **Curriculum**

10. **Division of Academic Affairs** vs. **Division of Student Affairs**

11. **Liberal Studies** or **Core Studies**

12. **Major** vs. **minor**

13. **Placement tests**

14. **Quality points & QPA; Cumulative Grade Point Average (CGPA)**

15. **Registrar**

16. **Semester hour load** and **overload**

17. **Syllabus**

18. **Transfer credits**

List of Institutional Contacts

For the chart below, fill in names as they apply to you and your institution.
Use the organizational chart on the next page as a reference. Is your college/university similar?

Your Institution: _____

	Name	Campus Address/Phone/E-mail
President		
Provost Academic Affairs Division		
Vice President Student Affairs Division		
College of my Major		
College – Dean		
College – Associate Dean		
Department of my Major		
Department Chairperson		
My Academic Advisor		
Others:		

— Post this completed list at your study desk for easy referral. —

ORGANIZATION of a UNIVERSITY

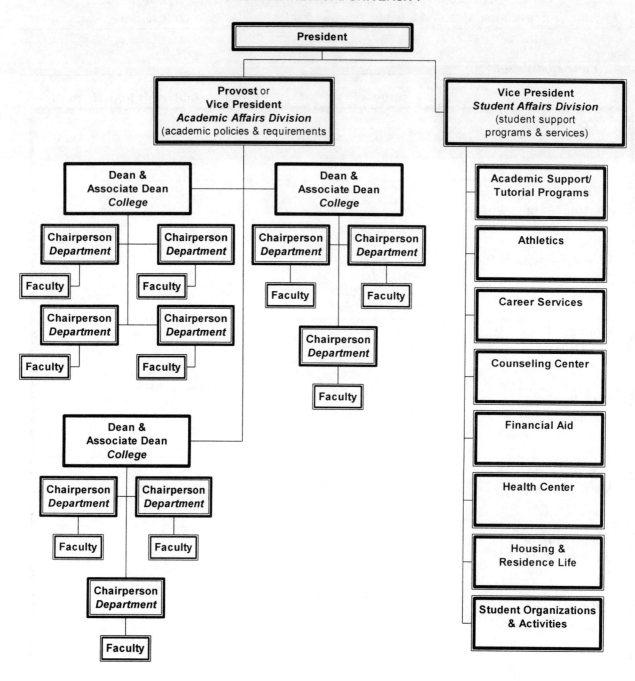

Academic Requirements: An Open Book Quiz

✓ Check with your instructor – this might be a group assignment.

A+

4.0

1. What is the minimum number of credit hours a student must complete in Liberal or Core Studies? _____

2. Is there a course that *all* students must complete before graduating? _____

3. How many credits must a student earn to attain sophomore standing? _____ Junior standing?_____ To graduate? _____

4. How many D/F repeats can a student take during the course of her college career?_____

5. How many Individual Course Withdrawals can a student take during the course of his college career? _____

6. What is the minimum Cumulative Grade Point Average a student must maintain to remain in Academic Good Standing? _____

7. In the fall semester, if a student earns the grades indicated, what will his fall grade point average be? *Show your work.*

Fall Schedule

College Writing	4 credits	Grade = B
History of the 20ᵗʰ Century	3 credits	Grade = A
Health & Wellness	3 credits	Grade = B
General Biology I	4 credits	Grade = C
Learning Strategies	1 credit	Grade = B

    Fall Semester GPA _____

8. In the spring term, if a student earns the grades indicated, what will his spring grade point average be? *Show your work.*

Spring Schedule

Humanities & Literature	3 credits	Grade = B
Foundations of Math	3 credits	Grade = A
Introduction to Theater	3 credits	Grade = D
General Biology II	4 credits	Grade = F
Career Exploration	1 credit	Grade = C
Geography of Non-Western World	3 credits	Grade = C

    Spring Semester GPA _____

9. What is this student's *first year CGPA?* _____

Beginning Your Curriculum Plan

*For this activity obtain an **undergraduate catalog** & a **curriculum guide** for your major/minor.*

What are the *requirements* for your major/minor in the following categories?
List your course options, as well as the semesters the courses usually are offered.

	Course Names/ #'s	*credit hrs*	Course Names/ #'s	*credit hrs*
English or **Writing**				
Fine Arts				
Health or **Physical Education**				
Humanities				
Languages				

	Course Names/ #'s	credit hrs	Course Names/ #'s	credit hrs
Mathematics				
Natural Sciences (include labs)				
Non-Western Cultures and/or **Synthesis**				
Social Sciences				
Electives				
Other				

Time to…

…and reflect.

Complete the following items:

A. Write a ***burning question*** that you have about your institution, your course of studies, or academic requirements.

B. In 2-4 sentences summarize the ***most useful information*** you have learned from the information & activities in this chapter.

CHAPTER 5: Developing Study Strategies

Study Reading

As a college student you likely will be assigned a greater amount and greater complexity of reading than you have previously experienced. Much of content-subject reading will consist of not only comprehending unfamiliar terms and ideas, but also analyzing and applying new information. As a college student you will be expected to independently read and absorb text information, often having to know material for an exam without having previously reviewed it in class. How can you best *understand* and *remember* reading assignments?

Before Reading:

Start with a plan about *how* you will approach a specific reading assignment. Consider the answers to these questions *before* reading a chapter or article:

1. **Why are you reading this selection? What are you going to *do* with the information?**

2. **How difficult do you expect the selection to be for you to understand? Why?**

3. **How long do you expect to take to read the selection?**

4. **When and where will you read? Will you break up your reading? Have you scheduled this assignment in your planner or weekly schedule?**

5. **How do you know that you understand the information? What can you do to remember the material? What type of study guide should you develop in order to maximize your understanding and remembering?** (Keep reading to learn more!)

Study Guides:

Create a study guide to increase your comprehension of text material. An effective study guide is one in which you *actively read* to:
- Select important ideas, and
- Organize and summarize these ideas.

Furthermore, use the study guide to periodically review text material. If you write ideas down as you read, you are more likely to understand and remember the information.

> 🔑 **Study guides are tools that guide you *to think while you read*.**
> ***Always* develop some type of study guide if you will be tested on what you are reading.**

Types of Study Guides

> ## Highlighting *and* Marking in the Book

This technique is especially appropriate if you need to know *many major and minor ideas.*

EXAMPLE:
⇓

One of the many challenges facing Supplemental Instruction (SI) Leaders is how to encourage students to attend sessions early, well before the first exam. Here are recommendations on how SI Leaders can have a positive impact on attendance: *** increase attendance SI ***

(1)   Actively seek participants for sessions. Be enthusiastic about what students can accomplish in an SI session; let students know you genuinely want them to attend. Remember: people often need a nudge before trying something new, such as SI—approach students before or after class, encouraging them to attend a specific session for the week. Remind students that SI is for everyone, not just those who are performing poorly; regular attendance enhances and eases study of course material. ↑ **import.**

(2)   Develop SI sessions with themes that are practical & immediate for the students. Be creative! By planning & publicizing these themes, you can "hook" students into coming to SI. One SI Leader notes: "I give the entire class periodic updates on what we will be working on. These serve as continuous reminders that SI is available." ↑ **ex.**

(3)   Develop a working relationship with the course professor. Initiate regular communication with the instructor—let him/her know how many students are attending SI Sessions (though not specific student names) **(a)** and what you have been working on in the sessions. If the instructor does not mention SI in class, ask him/her **(b)** to make a brief announcement encouraging students to attend (ALL students, not just those who did poorly on a **(c)** test). The more successful sessions tend to occur in subjects where professors openly support SI.

Being effective SI Leaders requires skills beyond knowing content. SI Leaders are the main catalyst for attendance; thus, they should be a visible and approachable presence for students *and* instructors. **Import SI ldr**

> ## Developing *and* Answering Questions

This technique will keep you focused on main ideas, especially with a *large quantity* of reading material→ make "*what*," "*how*," and "*why*" questions about key concepts.

EXAMPLE:
⇓

1) **How can SI Leaders increase attendance at sessions?**
2) **Why is it important for SI Leaders to communicate with the course instructor?**
3) **What is an example of an SI theme that might interest students?**
4) **Why is regular attendance at SI sessions important?**

➢ **Creating Study Cards**

A good choice if you need to know *terms*, including examples and applications.

EXAMPLE:
(Created by Kirsty Peyton for *Cell Biology*.)
⇓

FRONT	→	BACK
Microfilaments		Shape-*solid rods* Function-*muscles* *amoeba support*
Microtubules		Shape-*straight,* *hollow tubes* Function- *provides tracks* (ex) motion ✳→→nose/throat

FRONT → BACK

➢ **Outlining Key Ideas**

Carefully *select and paraphrase* important ideas.

EXAMPLE:
(Created by Erin Gattens for *General Psychology*.)
⇓

Memory
(i) Sensory Memory
  1. Properties:
    a. duration: very brief (e.g., <1 sec. for vision)
    b. capacity: very large
(ii) Short-Term Memory
  1. Properties
    a. duration: 1-30 sec.
    b. capacity: small (e.g. 7-9 items)
  2. Chunking
(iii) Long-Term Memory
  1. Properties
    a. duration: minutes to years
    b. capacity: very large
  2. From short-term to long-term
    a. primacy effect: more rehearsals of the first item
    b. recency effect: readily retrievable from short-term storage
  3. How information enters long-term storage
    a. elaborate rehearsal: simple repetition not sufficient
    b. levels of processing: superficial vs. deep processing

➤ **Developing a 'Map,' Chart, or Diagram**
Choose this technique if you learn best by *organizing or categorizing* key information into a *concise, visual summary.*

EXAMPLE:
(Created by Robin Eichenlaub for *Geoscience.*)
⇓

SEDIMENTARY ROCK

	Motion	Environment	Size of Sediment	Ex. of Sediment	
Moderate Energy Environment	Agitation and rapid motion	Strong waves, storms, floods, waterfalls	Large particles like GRAVEL	Breccia Jagged rock made of rock fragments	Conglo-merate rounded rock fragment
Moderate Energy Environment	Constant gentle motion	Rivers, beaches, deltas, windy, deserts	Medium grains like SAND	Sandstone quartz sand, f-spar, tiny rock fragments	
Low Energy Environment	Almost no motion	Lakes, swamps, deep oceans, flood plains	Very small grains like MUD	Shale Mud made of clay flakes- common around here	

EXAMPLE:
(Created by Erin Gattens for *General Psychology.*)
⇓

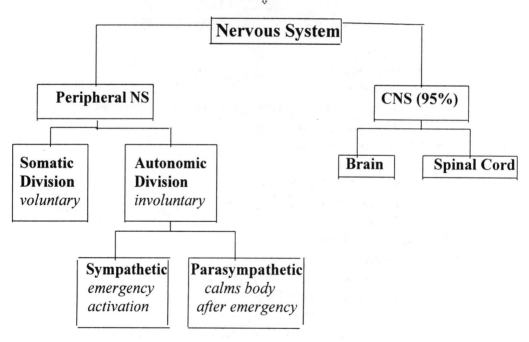

Application Assignment – Study Reading

✔ Check with your instructor – this might be a homework assignment.

Practice *study reading* with the following selection. Begin by answering the questions, choosing which type of study guide you will develop. Keep in mind that you will be using your study guide to review for a 5-point quiz!

1. **Why are you reading this selection? What are you going to *do* with the information?**

2. **How difficult do you expect the selection to be for you to understand? Why?**

3. **How long do you expect to take to read the selection?**

4. **When and where will you read?**

   Will you break up your reading?

   Have you scheduled this assignment in your planner?

5. **How do you know that you understand the information? What can you do to remember the material? What type of study guide should you develop in order to maximize your understanding and remembering?**

Keys to Effective Note Taking

The purpose of note taking is to help students listen to and understand lecture material. Good listening is an _active_ process, one that takes energy and thought on the students' part. Writing down everything the professor says is not good listening. Instead, as the professor talks about a subject, you should be thinking about what's important to know and writing down those pivotal ideas. The key to effective listening and note taking is to be _selective._ Lecture listening and note taking involves making decisions about what you do and do not need to write down.

One way to approach note taking is to think of a lecture as a professor's condensed version of a text chapter or several articles. That professor has chosen what material to present to the class. Likewise, your notes are a condensed version of a class lecture. You need to choose what material is important enough to be written in your notes. How do you make those decisions? Several factors come into play.

Ideas vs. Details

A common mistake that students make is to think that _everything_ is important, which results in students attempting to write down every word the professor says. Every word a professor says is not important. If your professor said the following sentence in class, what would you decide to write down on paper? Underline those words that seem important in order to get the idea across:

" _The little girl ran swiftly to the big, red barn._ "

You should have underlined, "girl ran to barn." Those few words are all that are needed to get the main idea across. The rest of the words in the above sentence are details that are secondary to the central idea. In order to be _selective_ about what you write in your notes, focus on main ideas.

Main ideas usually consist of two parts: the _topic or subject_ ("girl") plus _what you need to know about that topic._ If you are listening to a lecture and are having problems identifying the ideas being presented ask yourself these questions: "What is the professor talking about?" "What is important about that subject?"

Focusing in on main ideas should help you listen throughout a lecture. Of course, if you are not sure about an idea, ask the professor to explain. If you feel uncomfortable speaking up in class, put a question mark next to the material and ask the professor after class or find the information in your text.

Details are often needed to complete ideas in your notes. Use the details to explain or clarify ideas, not as material to be memorized on their own. Focus on details that are linked to main ideas and provide more meaning to the major concepts.

Writing your notes in phrases as opposed to whole sentences will help you focus in on concepts and ideas. You often do not need to write articles, adjectives, and adverbs in sentences. Concentrate on the two main parts of an idea – the subject *plus* what about that subject. This will add conciseness and speed to the note taking process.

Lecturer Cues

A cue is a signal, either verbal or nonverbal, that the lecturer gives you that something is important. Be aware – if your professor thinks a piece of information is important, it is likely that that information will be on the test. Therefore, you want to take notes on those things that your professor verbally or nonverbally emphasizes in class. Alertness to each professor's cues can aid you in being more selective with your note taking.

Verbal cues are things the professor says throughout the lecture that signify importance and, therefore, help you decide what information to write down. Examples are:

- *Repeating ideas* – If the professor takes the time to repeat something, it's probably because s/he thinks it is important and wants to make sure you get it down on paper.

- *Giving examples* – The professor is taking the time to explain an idea through the use of examples. Make sure you understand the idea that those examples are illustrating.

- *Asking questions* – Questions, such as "Do you understand this?" or "Am I making myself clear?" signal that the lecturer thinks the information is important and you should thoroughly understand it. Even if you do not answer these types of questions aloud, answer them to yourself. Do you understand? If "yes," place a mark next to the idea indicating importance; if "no," place a question mark next to the idea so that you can come back to it.

- *Use of signal or transitional phrases* – Similar to the questions, these phrases are not needed to get the meaning of the information across. However, they do serve a purpose to organize and, often times, emphasize ideas. Examples include: "Remember this..." and "The four causes of poor listening are: first... second... third... fourth." Be alert to these phrases for they can aid you in organizing and emphasizing the information in your notes.

- *Introducing or summarizing the lecture's main points* – At the beginning of a lecture a professor will often list the objectives or main points that s/he intends to present. Make note of these points, checking to make sure your notes cover them. Also, be aware of the end of a lecture when a professor often summarizes the points covered in the lecture. In addition, at the beginning and ending of lectures a professor will mention quizzes, tests, assignments, and so on. Be alert to this information.

- *Use of voice* – A lecturer often will emphasize important points through the volume and rate of his/her voice. A professor talking louder or at a slower rate can be a signal that s/he thinks something is important and wants to make sure you hear the information and have time to write it down.

Nonverbal cues are those non-speaking signals, such as body movements, that a professor provides indicating that something is important. Examples of nonverbal cues are:

- *Use of a blackboard, overhead projector, or handouts* – Again, if a professor is going to take the time to write something down and provide a visual emphasis for the class, it is probably important. Therefore, make sure that you write it down in your notes.

- *Use of hand gestures* – Hand gestures are used to emphasize points. This can include putting fingers up in the air to emphasize order of ideas, pounding on a lectern, or pointing to something written on the board.

- *Body and facial expressions* – Like hand gestures, other body movements can reflect the personalities and individual quirks of a professor. If you notice that a professor paces back and forth whenever s/he gets excited about a point, recognize that if the professor is excited about something, that information probably will be on the test. Body and facial expressions can indicate what information you should be selecting for your notes.

Developing a Method of Note Taking & Study

You will want to develop a style of note taking that keeps you actively involved in the process of selective listening, note taking, and study. There is no one 'best' method of note taking for all students, although certain methods tend to work better for the majority of students. As always, it is up to you to experiment with methods before deciding on a model that provides you with clear, complete, concise notes that you can effectively use for review and study. Four differing models are summarized:

I.   *Highlighting and Jotting* – This method is based upon the premise that you will go back over your notes as soon after class as possible. During that review, think about what is really important to know. Highlight key words and important phrases that you want to stand out within your notes. Use these words and phrases to refresh your memory during the weekly review. In addition, as you go through your notes, jot down ideas that you missed or phrases that can summarize a large section of material. Use colored pens or pencils to emphasize the jottings. Refer to the text to write down additional ideas that help explain or emphasize the lecture material. By highlighting and jotting down key points, you are *studying* your lecture material.

II.   *Developing Questions* – As you go back over your notes after class, develop questions for yourself that spotlight important ideas that you anticipate will be on an upcoming test. If you do not know what type of questions will be on the next test, ask your professor. Write the questions on a separate sheet of paper, in a column beside your lecture notes, or on note cards. Not only does this method make you think about what is important to know about the lecture material, but it also gives you the opportunity to identify and answer potential test questions. Thus, you gain confidence from knowing the material as well as from practicing how to answer questions about the material.

III.   *Making a Separate Column* – For this system you will need to leave a blank column on one side of your notebook paper. The pink line on the side of your paper sometimes provides a wide enough margin, especially if the paper does not have holes. Otherwise, draw a vertical line down the paper – on the left side, if you are right-handed; on the right side, if you are left-handed. *After* class create a study guide for yourself in this column. Go back over your lecture notes, think about what is important, then jot down key words, phrases, terms, and questions in the column. During your weekly review, cover up the main body of notes and use the jottings in the column to jog your memory as to what is important in your lecture notes.

IV.   *Two Columns: Lecture and Text* – This model is helpful if the lecture and text material closely correspond in a given course. Write lecture notes on one side of the paper. After class, go through the text material, jotting down further explanations and examples for the material presented in class. Sometimes you will need to write ideas that are not covered in class but likely will be on the test. This system is a great method for integrating lecture and text material.

End of Sample Reading Selection

Lecture Note Taking

The most prevalent format for college classes is the <u>lecture</u>. Many instructors, especially for large introductory courses, primarily present material by talking about it for the entire class time. As a college student, you can expect to encounter large amounts and a great complexity of information within a single class period. This is information that will be on tests and, therefore, information that you will want to *understand* and *remember*. Thus, as with your course readings, your primary goal will be to convert the passive act of 'listening' into a more active, involved activity.

🔑 ***Writing notes* while you are listening is an important strategy to keep you *actively involved* in a class.**

◆ Note taking keeps your mind <u>focused</u> on what the instructor is saying and doing;
◆ Note taking guides you to <u>think</u> about the information;
◆ Note taking assists you to <u>discover</u> what you *do* and *do not* know.

A key to active note taking is to be **selective** about what you write down on your paper. You want to achieve a balance – not writing too much information, that is, *everything* the instructor says; yet not writing too little, such as *only* what the instructor writes on the board. This balance is more likely to occur if you focus on **ideas** that are being presented. Keep asking yourself: "What are the important points that the instructor is trying to get across?" Then write down enough information to help you understand those points.

Effective class notes have the following characteristics:

1) **Conciseness** – You want to use as few words as possible to represent key ideas. Speed is an element in class notes. You need to write down ideas quickly, especially if you are encountering a lot of information or if your instructor talks very fast. Some pointers are:
   - *Write in phrases*, not whole sentences.
   - *Use abbreviations and symbols*.
   - *Use paper wisely* – Leave amble spaces between ideas or when you are missing information.
   - *Use a pen* to help you write smoother and quicker.
2) **Clarity** – You want your notes to be clear enough for you to read and understand <u>after</u> class.
3) **Correctness** – You want the ideas to be represented accurately within your notes. To ensure correctness:
   - Review your notes *after class*.
   - Refer to your *textbook*.
   - Go over class information in *study groups*, *Supplemental Instruction*, or *tutorial appointments*.

Study Guides for Class Notes:

🔑 **Reviewing notes and creating a study guide <u>soon after class</u> is pivotal for understanding and remembering class information.**

<u>Study guides</u> for class notes are similar to the types of study guides for class readings presented earlier in this chapter.
- **Highlighting** *and* **marking key words and phrases within your class notes.**
- **Developing** *and* **answering questions about class information.**
- **Creating study cards from the information presented in class.**
- **Developing a 'map', chart, or diagram that organizes and summarizes class information.**

Application Assignment – Lecture Note Taking

In order to practice taking notes and developing a study guide, your instructor will present a mock lecture. You will need lined paper and a pen. As you listen to your instructor's lecture, write down the key ideas. Afterwards, go back through your notes and evaluate what you have written by referring to the characteristics of effective notes presented on the previous page:

1) **Are your notes concise?**

2) **Are your notes clear enough for you to read and understand?**

3) **Are your notes correct? Did you represent ideas accurately?**

Using your notes from the mock lecture, create one of the four types of study guides listed above. (Your instructor might assign you a particular format for your study guide.) Keep in mind that your study guide is a means by which you can review your notes and check for your understanding of the material.

✔ Check with your instructor – this might be a group activity.

Get feedback about your study guide from others in the class. Critique each other's study guides:

1) **Is the study guide a summary of important points?**

2) **Is the study guide comprehensive enough? ...or is it *too* comprehensive?**

3) **Is the study guide easy to read and understand?**

4) **Is the study guide an effective tool for review before a quiz or test?**

CHAPTER 6: Connecting with the Campus Community

This information relates to *Getting Involved in Campus Life*, the mock lecture for Chapter 5.

The Importance of 'Connecting'

Consider your college or university as a "community," that is, an organization composed of buildings and people with a variety of common goals, plans, and interests. As a new member of this community, you will need time to feel comfortable and find your 'fit' within the various components of college life, including activities extending beyond classes and homework. You will become more at ease with your day-to-day life as a college student as you become acquainted with other members of the campus community – classmates, roommates, professors, and staff members – and more accustomed to expectations and routines. You will benefit greatly if, from the start, you explore the campus jobs, organizations, and activities related to your experiences and interests.

> Students who participate in a range of campus activities within their college community tend to *perform better academically* and be *more satisfied* with their college experience.

Therefore, connect with at least one area of campus life your first semester! From there, you can add or modify as your academic, personal, and social needs develop and change throughout your college career. The information on the following pages will assist you with making decisions on *where* and *how* to seek out campus connections.

Types of Connections

Involvement in the campus community can take a variety of forms. Consider what your institution offers within these three categories of activities: **academic, personal,** and **social**.

Academic Activities: Participation in activities oriented towards academics will improve your performance in courses, offer you insight and direction in choices for your major and career, and provide you with valuable social connections. Furthermore, academic support services, such as those listed below, usually are <u>free</u>! Therefore, discover what academic support services are offered at your institution.

❑ **Library** – Become familiar with the layout of your library, including:
- ⇨ **Reference desk,**
- ⇨ **Circulation area,**
- ⇨ **Periodicals,**
- ⇨ **Media resources,**
- ⇨ **Special collections, and**
- ⇨ **Photocopying and special services.**

   Also, search for appropriate **study locations** in the library for yourself (such as study carrels) and for a group of students (such as private study rooms). Find out if you need to reserve these locations in advance.

❑ **Student Academic Support Services** – Your campus Learning Center or Academic Support Center offers valuable academic services. Often upper class peers are hired and trained to assist fellow students in a variety of ways:
- ⇨ **Peer Tutoring** for individual work with difficult assignments or class work.
- ⇨ **Study Skills Workshops** for information on college success strategies.
- ⇨ **Supplemental Instruction** for small-group assistance with difficult courses.
- ⇨ **Writing Center** for help with composing, writing, editing, revising/rewriting of papers.

   Students who *regularly* use academic support services, such as those listed above, *earn higher final grades in their course work.* Therefore, join other students in utilizing these services → you will be strengthening your *social network*, as well as your *grades*!

❑ **Career Services** – Provides information on:
- ⇨ **Careers options,**
- ⇨ **Job hunting techniques** and **companies,**
- ⇨ **Job listings** – both on-campus and off-campus,
- ⇨ **Resume writing,**
- ⇨ **Mock interviews**, and
- ⇨ **Career-related workshops**, such as "Dress for Success," or "Tips for Interviewing."

❑ **Major Departments** – Academic departments have activities, such as:
- ⇨ **Competitions with other colleges** (such as Computer Science Programming Team),
- ⇨ **Societies** or **Councils** (such as Political Science Council and Pre-Law Society),
- ⇨ **Discipline-related organizations** (such as Spanish Club and Education Association), &
- ⇨ **Professional Development**, including opportunities to attend local, state, or national conferences.

Personal Activities relate to your mental, physical, and/or economic well-being and include:

❑ **Counseling and Support Groups**
  ⇨ **Campus Counseling Center** provides individual or group counseling & support groups (such as for eating disorders or gay/lesbian support groups).
  ⇨ **Campus Health Center** provides education about alcohol abuse & sexual relationships.
  ⇨ **Off-Campus Support** consists of organizations such as Alcoholics Anonymous and Victims of Violence.

❑ **Campus Jobs** – Work-study jobs usually are posted at a central location on campus, such as the Career Services Office, Financial Aid Office, or Student Union. However, campus job openings often are not officially listed – you must go around to offices, departments, or professors and *ask* about openings. Examples of campus jobs are:
  ⇨ **Department office workers**,
  ⇨ **Dining hall workers**,
  ⇨ **Peer tutors or educators**,
  ⇨ **Library aids**,
  ⇨ **Recreational facilities staff**,
  ⇨ **Athletics offices** and **team sports staff**,
  ⇨ **Residence hall assistants**, and
  ⇨ **Campus tour guides**.

Extracurricular Activities: By meeting others with interests and purposes similar to your own, extracurricular organizations can provide you with a compatible social network. Furthermore, these organizations can offer you a range of enriching experiences and responsibilities, all of which will strengthen your future resume!

❑ **Recognized Programs and Organizations** – Go to the campus-wide *Activity Fair* at beginning of the academic year. Look for clubs or organizations that relate to your major or interests. Talk to members of the organizations. See if you can pinpoint at least one organization that you will join your first year.

❑ **Intramural Sports** – Join an intramural team or use the campus recreational/fitness facilities. Your involvement demonstrates teamwork, as well as your ability to balance school work and recreation.

❑ **Religious and Ethnic or Cultural Organizations** – Organizations, such as the African American Cultural Center, the Women's Center, or religious congregations, provide students with a support network within the campus community.

In conclusion, by participating in one or more of these campus wide activities, you will be exposing yourself to a wide range of opportunities and experiences. Furthermore, as you build a supportive and compatible social network for yourself, you will be establishing your place in the campus community and, thus, providing yourself with a '*home away from home*'!

Exploring Campus Organizations

A list of categorizes for various types of campus student organizations follows. Check those represented at your institution; then write two additional examples for each category.

❑ **Department-related or Subject-related Organizations**
   Examples: *Business Club; Society for Financial Planners*

   Other examples: _____

❑ **Campus Governing Organizations**
   Examples: *Student Congress; Residence Hall Council*

   Other examples: _____

❑ **Campus Programming Committees & Organizations**
   Examples: *Homecoming Committee; Student Entertainment Committee; Marching Band*
   Other examples: _____

❑ **Community or Campus Service Organizations**
   Examples: *Big Brothers & Big Sisters; Volunteers for the Elderly*

   Other examples: _____

❑ **Greek Organizations**
   Examples: *Sigma Kappa* (Sorority); *Sigma Chi* (Fraternity)

   Other examples: _____

❑ **Honorary Societies**
   Example: *Pi Omega Pi* (Business)

   Other examples: _____

❑ **Professional Fraternities**
   Example: *Phi Gamma Nu* (Business/Economics)

   Other examples: _____

❑ **Recreational & Sports Organizations**
   Example: *Ski Club; Intramural Volleyball*

   Other examples: _____

❑ **Religious Organizations**
   Examples: *Campus Ministry; Hillel Association*

   Other examples: _____

❑ **Special Interest Organizations**
   Examples: *Commuter Student Club; Campus Choir; Student Democratic Club*

   Other examples: _____

Answer these questions about student organizations:

1) **At your institution, what campus office oversees student organizations?**

2) **At your institution, is there a difference between 'recognized' and 'unrecognized' student organizations?   If so, what is the difference?**

3) **Do student organizations have a faculty or administrative advisor at your institution?**

4) **What is the procedure for becoming involved in an organization at your campus?**

5) **What organizations would you like to become involved in during your first year?** *List your top 3 choices and the name, address, & phone number of the person to contact about joining.*

#1 _____

*contact person:*_____

#2 _____

*contact person:*_____

#3 _____

*contact person:*_____

Professors as Resources

View each of your instructors as a valuable resource; that is, someone who can guide you through the subject matter and requirements for that particular class. In addition, consider professors as future contacts for references, information, and assistance.

Your behavior and demeanor in a classroom is the first impression by which an instructor will judge you. Keep in mind that each of your instructors will be evaluating your performance throughout the semester. Since you want to earn a high grade in the course, it is in your best interest to adapt to each professor's style and expectations. Showing your 'best' behavior and attitude in a class setting will greatly benefit you as a student.

➢ **AVOID**: *Passive behaviors*, such as
    1) Looking around the room (as opposed to making eye contact with the professor),
    2) Not writing class notes,
    3) Appearing disinterested or bored,
    4) Not participating in class, or
    5) Coming to class unprepared & leaving your text and assignments at home.

➢ **AVOID**: *Disruptive or distracting behaviors*, such as
    1) Talking to classmates while the professor is lecturing,
    2) Challenging the professor in a mean-spirited manner,
    3) Consistently entering the classroom late or leaving the room early, or
    4) Bringing a meal to class.

➢ **DEMONSTRATE**: *Active behaviors and attitudes*, such as (<u>*fill in the blanks*</u>):
    1)

    2)

    3)

    4)

🔑 **The best way to utilize your professor as a resource person is to meet with each professor throughout the semester or term. At the start of each term write down the following information about the instructor for each of your courses:**

    1) Name, including proper title (Dr., Mr., Mrs., Ms.)
    2) Office location, phone #, e-mail address
    3) Office Hours—Instructors usually post the days and times during the week that they will be in their offices. Although instructors have regular office hours, without an appointment you cannot count on them being available to meet with you. Avoid dropping in unannounced during office hours.
    It is best to schedule an appointment ahead of time with the instructor.

Meeting with a Professor

🔎 **Arrive promptly for your meeting with the instructor.** *If for some reason you are late or cannot make the scheduled appointment,* **contact the professor as soon as you can.**

🔎 **Come to your appointment prepared with specific questions for the professor to answer.** Think about what you want to focus on during this appointment. This is especially helpful if you are intimidated at the idea of meeting one-on-one with a professor.

Questions for a Meeting at the Beginning of the Term:

❏ Show your professor your class notes. Do your notes seem complete and accurate? Can your professor suggest ways for you to improve your notes?

❏ Show your professor how you presently read course material. Does your professor have suggestions about how you can improve your understanding of the text material?

❏ Does you professor have any other suggestions for how to best study and review the course content?

❏ Does your professor have supplemental study questions or practice tests to help you prepare for exams?

Questions for a Meeting at the Middle of the Term:

❏ Ask you professor to rate your performance thus far according to:
  ✓ Quizzes and exams.

  ✓ Papers.

  ✓ Projects.

  ✓ Homework assignments.

  ✓ Your class participation.

  ✓ Your class attendance.

  ✓ Any other outstanding measures.

❏ What is your mid-term grade for the course?

❏ What can the professor recommend that you do to improve your grade?

❏ Does your professor recommend that you seek tutorial or other help for course content?

Questions for a Meeting Near the End of the Term:

❏ What suggestions can your professor give you to prepare for the final exam?

❏ What is your grade for the course at this point?

❏ Do you have any outstanding assignments for the course?

❏ Are extra credit assignments available to improve your grade?

Scenarios to Solve:

(Contributed by Jessica Mayhugh.)

✓ Check with your instructor – this might be a group assignment.

#1: One of your instructors has office hours at the same time that you have another class. You have a question that you want answered. What are your options?

#2: After the first week of class you realize that a course will be very challenging for you. How can your professor assist you?

#3: Your professor rushed through some complex, confusing material during the previous class session. You have no idea what you wrote down in your notes. How do you prepare to meet with your professor to review the class material?

#4: You go to see an instructor on a regular basis, but you *still* are struggling with class material. What are your options?

CHAPTER 7: Examining Policies & Procedures

Focus Questions: Student Policies

✓ Check with your instructor – this likely is a group assignment.

As a beginning student you will want to be familiar with the policies and procedures specific to your college or university. You likely will find academic policies and procedures in your **Undergraduate Catalog**, and/or **Student Handbook**.

The following pages present questions concerning the key policies presented below. (Note that some policies and accompanying questions might not be appropriate for your institution.)

- **Academic Good Standing**

- **Grading & Attendance Policies**

- **Withdrawal Policy**

- **Academic Integrity Policy**

- **Student Behavior Standards**

- **Alcohol Policy**

- **Hazing Policy**

- **Judicial Systems**

Your instructor will tell you how many of these worksheets to complete. Also, if you come across information about other policies or requirements, write down this information to share with others in your class!

Academic Good Standing

Group Questions:

1. How is *Academic Good Standing* defined?

2. Discuss the *end-of-semester* and *end-of-year* academic review periods.

3. What is the definition of *Academic Probation*?

4. What is the definition of *Academic Honors?*

Grading & Attendance Policies

Group Questions:

1. What is the grading system at your institution? How are grades calculated?

2. a. Is there a *Grade Appeal Policy*?   If so, what is it?

   b. On what grounds may a student initiate this process?

   c. What are the steps taken?

3. Is there a *Class Attendance Policy*?   If so, what is it?

Withdrawal Policy

Group Questions:

1. How many *individual course withdrawals* are permitted?

2. What is the deadline for processing an *individual course withdrawal*?

3. How do you process an *individual course withdrawal*?

4. What is the difference between an *individual course withdrawal* and a *total university withdrawal*?

Academic Integrity Policy

Group Questions:

1. Does your institution have an academic integrity policy?   If so, define the policy.

Don't students know what plagiarism is?

2. Give examples of three violations.

3. Give examples of sanctions attached to violating this policy.
   Include mild to extreme scenarios.

Student Behavior Standards

Group Questions:

1. Is there a standard for student behavior at your institution?
   If so, what is the intent of this standard?

2. What does this standard allow the university to do?

3. Identify the behaviors and/or actions that are prohibited at your institution.

NO DRUGS

NO ALCOHOL

NO VIOLENCE

Alcohol Policy

Group Questions:

1. Does your institution have a policy regarding alcohol?   If so, what is it?

2. What is the legal age to consume alcohol?

3. What are the possible consequences for violating the alcohol policy at your institution?

4. What risks do college students face related to alcohol use/abuse and binge drinking?

Hazing Policy

Fraternity or Sorority House

Group Questions:

1. What is the definition of *hazing*?

2. Give specific examples of what the hazing policy includes.

3. Give examples of sanctions attached to the hazing policy.

Judicial Systems

Group Questions:

1. Identify the types of *judicial systems* at your institution.

2. Who can press charges and to whom do you report those charges?

3. What are the general guidelines for judicial hearings?

4. Identify a range of sanctions that may be imposed.

Time to …

…and reflect.

Complete the following items:

A. Write a *burning question* that you have at this point.

B. In 2-4 sentences summarize the *most useful information* you have learned about the policies and procedures within your institution.

CHAPTER 8: Solving Problems & Setting Goals

Steps for Solving Problems: Case Studies

With the many academic, social, and personal changes happening during your first year of college, it is almost inevitable that new and unexpected difficulties will occur. To better prepare yourself for these difficulties, consider how other students have tackled new, difficult, and/or perplexing situations. The following is a list of <u>five recommended steps</u> to refer to when faced with a challenging situation or problem:

1. **Be positive – identify the problem and view it as an opportunity or challenge!**

2. **List all possible causes. Then eliminate those that you can and prioritize the rest.**

3. **List all possible solutions. Prioritize from most appropriate to least appropriate.**

4. **Begin solution #1 as soon as possible – listing steps, resources, and a timeline.**

5. **Evaluate your performance, making needed adjustments.**

Practice applying these five steps by solving the academic problems of students described below.

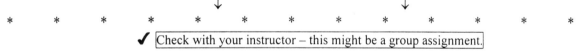

✓ Check with your instructor – this might be a group assignment.

Identify the main problem and at least <u>three</u> recommendations for each case. For specific strategies refer to previous assignments, including the "Checklist for Active Decision-Making" on page 18.

Case #1 – JASON:

Jason complains that he just cannot remember what he reads in his textbook for the <u>History of the Modern Era</u> course. The chapters are long (30-40 pages each) and "boring" according to Jason. The professor assigns a chapter per week, with a 75-point essay exam covering the text material every five weeks. Presently, Jason is in the habit of beginning to read the weekly chapter every Thursday evening after watching <u>E.R.</u> on television. Although he uses a highlighter and has plenty of pink pages, Jason complains that he quickly loses concentration when reading.

Jason's Problem:

Recommended Solution:

Case #2 – ARIEL:

Ariel insists that she does not have enough hours in the day to complete all of her schoolwork. She is taking 15 credit-hours of classes, is employed for 15 hours per week at Pizza Hut, has a boyfriend 150 miles away that she talks to daily and sees on weekends, is pledging a sorority, is an avid fan of All My Children and Days of Our Lives, and enjoys socializing with the dozen other freshmen on her floor of the residence hall.

Ariel's Problem:

Recommended Solution:

Case #3 – CHRIS:

Chris is enrolled in a General Psychology class with about 75 other students. The three hours of class each week consist entirely of lecture, with 100-point, multiple-choice tests (primarily covering lecture material) twice during the term. Given that the class begins at 8:00 a.m., *if* Chris shows up for class he rushes out of bed and invariably arrives late, sliding into a seat at the rear of the auditorium. Chris frantically tries to write everything the professor is saying, but often has big gaps in his lecture notes. After class Chris closes his notebook until the next class session.

Chris' Problem:

Recommended Solution:

Developing Personal Goals

You will be determining your academic path in college by taking responsibility for your successes *and* failures in school. This mission of self-determination begins at the start of your academic career. A recognition of *where you intend to be* and *what you intend to do* in the short term (i.e. today) and long term (i.e. four years) can bring about the needed <u>action</u> on your part.

A **Goal Statement** is a written plan of ***where* you intend to be** or ***what* you intend to do**, and ***how* you intend to get there**. A Goal Statement is a *realistic commitment* to *yourself* for *action*. Goal Statements consist of specific, manageable steps that motivate you to act.

By setting goals for yourself, you will be monitoring your successes and failures and learning through trial-and-error. Your first year in college will be full of changes – goals provide a means to periodically assess your academic, social, and personal directions.

<u>Examples of Short-Term Goals</u> → <u>Which Goal Statement is the best?</u>   <u>Why?</u>

    A. I intend to study psychology for one hour after lunch each weekday.

    B. I pledge to improve my concentration this week.

    C. I'll try to listen better to my history professor's lectures.

<u>Examples of Long-Term Goals</u> → <u>Which Goal Statement is the best?</u>   <u>Why?</u>

    A. I intend to get "A's" in all my courses this term.

    B. I'll probably do better spring term than I will fall term.

    C. I intend to decide on a major by the end of my freshman year.

Two formats for Goal Statements are provided on the following workbook pages:
- **Goal Statements – 6 Steps**, and
- **Goal Statements – 4 Steps**.

❑ Use these pages to practice developing your own Goal Statements for:
  1) **The upcoming week**,
  2) **Your freshman year**, and
  3) **Four+ years from now**.

> ✔ Check with your instructor – this might be a homework assignment.

❑ Ask yourself the following questions about each Goal Statement that you developed:
  1) **Is the Goal Statement *exact*?**
  2) **Is the Goal Statement *realistic* – will I likely follow through with it?**
  3) **Is the Goal Statement *meaningful to me*?**

Evaluating Your Goals

Practice referring to and reflecting about your goal. At the end of the time frame, evaluate what happened. Use this information in developing your next Goal Statement. Your answers to the following questions will guide you in assessing the effectiveness of your Goal Statement. Start with the Goal Statement that you developed for the "Upcoming Week."

1. **How worthwhile was your Goal Statement?**

2. **Did you follow through with your intentions, either wholly or partly?**

3. **Did the anticipated obstacles occur and, if so, were you able to overcome the obstacles?**

4. **What other obstacles did you discover?**

5. **Did you reward yourself?**

6. **Was the time frame appropriate?**

Expect that your first Goal Statement will not work out exactly as anticipated. Adjusting to college life often requires trial-and-error; it is inevitable that you will not always succeed when trying new things. However, do learn from your attempts. Three common missteps with Goal Statements are:

➤ **Taking too big a step when building a Goal Statement**. Students often develop goals that are either too general ("I intend to improve my time management") or too unrealistic ("I intend to study in the library for two hours every night this week").

➤ **Misjudging potential obstacles and how to overcome these obstacles**. For example, a student might anticipate that the greatest obstacle will be the temptation to turn on the television. However, after moving to another study location, the student realizes that lack of concentration is actually the greatest obstacle.

➤ **Not identifying an appropriate and meaningful reward**. Examine whether you rewarded yourself with something, whether internal or external, that *you* want – and can have!

Goal Statements – 6 Steps

1. I intend to:

2. I will accomplish this by the following means or steps:

3. The biggest obstacle to accomplishing this will be:

4. I will overcome this obstacle by:

5. My reward for accomplishing this will be:

6. The time frame for accomplishing this is:

---

1. I intend to:

2. I will accomplish this by the following means or steps:

3. The biggest obstacle to accomplishing this will be:

4. I will overcome this obstacle by:

5. My reward for accomplishing this will be:

6. The time frame for accomplishing this is:

Evaluate each goal statement by completing these questions:

1. How worthwhile was your Goal Statement?

2. Did you follow through with your intentions either wholly or partly?

3. Did the anticipated obstacles occur and, if so, were you able to overcome the obstacles?

4. What other obstacles did you discover?

5. Did you reward yourself?

6. Was the time frame appropriate?

---

1. How worthwhile was your Goal Statement?

2. Did you follow through with your intentions either wholly or partly?

3. Did the anticipated obstacles occur and, if so, were you able to overcome the obstacles?

4. What other obstacles did you discover?

5. Did you reward yourself?

6. Was the time frame appropriate?

Goal Statements – 4 Steps

I. Write an academic goal statement about something you need to accomplish in a course. Set a deadline. This should be a short-term goal.

II. Identify the steps you will take to implement and complete your goal. What will you *do*? Use one to three steps.

    1.

    2.

    3.

III. <u>Before</u> you begin the implementation of your goal, create a grid outlining your steps and completion timeline. This further documents your intention and provides you with a visual aid to monitor your progress. An example of a student's grid is below:

DATES ⇒ STEPS ⇓	9/5	9/7	9/12	9/14	9/18 day before quiz
1. take notes from chapters					
2. recite notes w/ roommate					
3. review notes at SI					

As you complete each of your steps along the timeline, give yourself a checkmark. Leave unattended dates/steps blank.

IV. At the conclusion of your allotted time period, answer the following questions:

    1. Did you carry out your goal as planned?

    2. What were the results?

    3. Given your results, what did you learn or discover about yourself?

    4. How will you use this feedback in determining your next goal for this course?

Evaluate your goal statement by completing these questions:

1. How worthwhile was your Goal Statement?

2. Did you follow through with your intentions either wholly or partly?

3. Did the anticipated obstacles occur and, if so, were you able to overcome the obstacles?

4. What other obstacles did you discover?

5. Did you reward yourself?

6. Was the time frame appropriate?

You – as a Problem Solver!

What will be your biggest stumbling block in completing your first year of college? Apply Steps to Problem Solving (page 69) to work through the process. Proceed step by step. Identify each step before writing your response.

You – as the Goal Setter!

A. List the courses on your schedule. What grade do you expect to earn in each course? Set goals! Given *your expected grades*, calculate *your end-of-term GPA*. Show your work.

Course Title:	Credits:	Expected Final Grade:	Grade Point Average:

B. Develop a *short-term academic goal* for the course you expect to be the most challenging for you. Select one of the goal action plans, either 6 steps (page 73) or 4 steps (page 75), identifying each step before writing your response.

CHAPTER 9: A Focus on the Future

Your first year of college will be full of opportunities and changes. You will be laying the foundation for the rest of your college career. In the upcoming semesters you will build upon the decisions, strategies, and attitudes that you implement _now_.

Five principles for college success are listed on the following chart. Think of these principles as yardsticks by which to measure your performance as a student – use them to gauge your progress through the upcoming semesters.

I.   **Begin now to assess yourself by completing the column labeled:**

> ### _What does this mean to me as a student?_

⇨ **How do you personally <u>define</u> each principle?**

⇨ **Consider how each principle is reflected in your day-to-day life?**

⇨ **Can you think of <u>examples</u> that are meaningful to you?**

Then...

II.   **Each semester assess your performance for the five principles. Write the date and your answers on the lines in the column labeled:**

> ### _Am I accomplishing this?_

⇨ **Jot down new behaviors and attitudes that reflect your success with college life.**

By periodically reflecting on these five principles, you will be focusing your attention on standards for success, not only for this year, but also for the rest of your college career!

— **Principles for College Success** —

	What does this mean to me as a student?	Am I accomplishing this?
Be Self-Directed Towards Goals.		
Be Organized.		
Be Prepared.		
Be Motivated.		
Be Persistent.		

Principles for College Success

	Am I accomplishing this?
Be Self-Directed Towards Goals.	
Be Organized.	
Be Prepared.	
Be Motivated.	
Be Persistent.	